P9-BZL-494

SONGS FOR THE OPEN ROAD
POEMS OF TRAVEL & ADVENTURE

DOVER THRIFT EDITIONS

Edited by
The American
Poetry & Literacy Project

DOVER PUBLICATIONS, INC.
MINEOLA, NEW YORK

DOVER THRIFT EDITIONS

GENERAL EDITOR: PAUL NEGRI
EDITORS OF THIS VOLUME

ANDREW CARROLL
DONALD MACLEAN

ASSOCIATE EDITORS

SUNIL IYENGAR
GEORGE DANIEL PATTERSON
ELIZABETH ELAM ROTH

Bibliographical Note

Songs for the Open Road is a new work, first published by Dover Publications, Inc., in 1999.

Library of Congress Cataloging-in-Publication Data

Songs for the open road : poems of travel and adventure / edited by the American Poetry & Literacy Project.
    p. cm.
  ISBN-13: 978-0-486-40646-6 (pbk.)
  ISBN-10: 0-486-40646-6 (pbk.)
   1. Travel—Poetry. 2. Adventure and adventurers—Poetry. 3. Voyages and travels—Poetry 4. American poetry 5. English poetry. I. American Poetry & Literacy Project (Mineola, N.Y.).

PS595.T75S66 1999
811.008'.0355—dc21

98-49683
CIP

Manufactured in the United States by LSC Communications
40646621   2020
www.doverpublications.com

Poetry Is Motion

THE CALL COMES FROM SOMEWHERE DEEP WITHIN US: Embark. Set sail. Venture forth. Head out. Escape. Drive. Fly. Steal away. *Just go.*

And we can't help but listen. We are restless creatures at heart, and the impulse to leave the comforts of home to explore distant and exotic realms wells up from the core of our being. This book is a celebration of that desire, that irrepressible urge not merely to get somewhere, but to experience the exhilaration of the journey itself. It is the "rapture" that Byron exalts before departing on his famous pilgrimage, the "lull of the wheels" Gene Zeiger describes in her ode to the highway, and the thrill of anticipation that "sets the gypsy blood astir" in Bliss Carman's "A Vagabond Song."

Few mediums convey this spirit of movement and discovery more passionately than poetry. Poems are journeys of the imagination, illuminating the unknown, enlivening the senses, and expanding our vistas and viewpoints. Poetry and travel not only introduce us to people, places, and cultures once foreign to us, they prompt us to reconsider familiar sights from a new perspective. "The end of our exploring," T. S. Eliot observes, "Will be to arrive where we started/And know the place for the first time." Ultimately we come away from poems and voyages alike with a keener eye and greater awareness of the world's endless and often breathtaking beauty.

From rollicking, devil-may-care narrations of peril and intrigue to more pensive meditations on soulful wandering, this collection strives to showcase a diversity of voices on the theme of travel. Robert Service's vibrant verse glorifies roaming alone and unfettered over frozen tundras and blistering deserts for the sheer stimulation of it. "From the red-rimmed star to the speck of sand,/From the vast to the greatly small," Service rhapsodizes, "For I know that the whole for good is planned,/And I want to see it all." (Service was true to his word: he trekked to the

Yukon, among many other inhospitable regions, and endured every conceivable hardship with undaunted vigor.)

Edna St. Vincent Millay experiences a similar rush whenever she hears the shriek of a train whistle; "[T]here isn't a train I wouldn't take," she exclaims, "No matter where it's going." For Henry Wadsworth Longfellow, it is the lure of waves and water that proves most seductive. "[M]y soul is full of longing/For the secret of the sea," Longfellow writes, "And the heart of the great ocean/Sends a thrilling pulse through me." And Walt Whitman, whose "Song of the Open Road" inspired this book's title, instructs travelers in another poem how best to maximize their wild and roving adventures: "Remember, fear not, be candid, promulge the body and the soul,/Dwell a while and pass on, be copious, temperate, chaste, [and] magnetic." Wise if enigmatic words.

Other poets in the collection follow a more subdued route, contemplating odysseys of mind and soul. E. E. Cummings traverses the geography of the heart in his love poem "somewhere i have never travelled,gladly beyond," while Robert Frost reflects on the mysteries of being "acquainted with the night" as he strolls beyond "the furthest city light." (Frost later muses, in a more well-known poem, on "the road not taken.") And James A. Emanuel explores the nature of sorrow and inspiration in his soaring "Get up, Blues," where he exhorts the human spirit to "Fly" and "Learn what it means/To be up high." Poems are points of departure, and through their words and sounds and images we take flight without ever leaving earth. As Emily Dickinson reminds us, "There is no frigate like a book,/to take us lands away."

Or to bring us back home. Even the most enthusiastic traveler recognizes that at some point there comes a time to return and—even if momentarily—rest and recharge. Thoughts of home invoke profound and powerful sentiments, and the poets in this anthology express a range of emotions, from the buoyantly patriotic to the inconsolably homesick. "Breathes there the man with soul so dead," asks Sir Walter Scott, "Whose heart hath ne'er within him burned/As home his footsteps he hath turned?" Claude McKay is seized with an almost unbearable memory of his native Jamaica after noticing a New York shop window abundant with mangoes, bananas, cocoa pods, and pears; "A wave of longing through my body swept," McKay grieves, "And, hungry for the old familiar ways,/I turned aside and bowed my head and wept." A. E. Housman concludes on a somber note as well, surmising of his travels: "That is the land of lost content,/I see it shining plain,/The happy highways where I went/And cannot come again."

But for those most stricken with the wanderlust, it isn't long before the romance of the road—or the sky or the sea or the rails—beckons once again. It is a compulsion that nothing, not even age, can diminish or restrain. "Come, my friends,/'Tis not too late to seek a newer world," an elderly king beseeches his old seafaring crew in Alfred, Lord Tennyson's "Ulysses." "[T]hough/We are not now that strength which in old days/Moved earth and heaven, that which we are, we are—/One equal temper of heroic hearts,/Made weak by time and fate, but strong in will/To strive, to seek, to find, and not to yield."

Ulysses' invitation to his men is Tennyson's call to us. Embark. Set sail. Venture forth. Head out. Escape. Drive. Fly. Steal away. *Just go.*

ANDREW CARROLL
Executive Director,
The American Poetry & Literacy Project

DONALD MACLEAN
Co-Editor, *Songs for the Open Road*

Acknowledgments

Helen Bevington: "The Journey Is Everything", from A CHANGE OF SKY by Helen Bevington. Copyright © 1950, 1951, 1952, 1954, 1955, 1956 by Helen Bevington. Reprinted by permission of Houghton Mifflin Company. All rights reserved.

Elizabeth Bishop: "Song" from THE COMPLETE POEMS 1927–1979 by Elizabeth Bishop. Copyright © 1979, 1983 by Alice Helen Methfessel. Reprinted by permission of Farrar, Straus & Giroux, Inc.

William Stanley Braithwaite: "Golden Moonrise", from SELECTED POEMS by William Stanley Braithwaite. Copyright 1948 by William Stanley Braithwaite, copyright renewed © 1975 by Katherine K. Arnold and Arnold D. Braithwaite. Used by permission of Coward-McCann, Inc., a division of Penguin Putnam, Inc.

Malcolm Cowley: "The Long Voyage", from BLUE JUNIATA: A LIFE by Malcolm Cowley. Copyright © 1985 by Malcolm Cowley. Used by permission of Viking Penguin, a division of Penguin Putnam, Inc.

E. E. Cummings: "what is", copyright © 1960, 1988, 1991 by the Trustees for the E. E. Cummings Trust. "somewhere i have never travelled,gladly beyond", copyright 1931, © 1959, 1991 by the Trustees for the E. E. Cummings Trust. Copyright © 1979 by George James Firmage, from COMPLETE POEMS: 1904–1962 by E. E. Cummings. Edited by George J. Firmage. Reprinted by permission of Liveright Publishing Corporation.

Stephen Dunn: "The Sacred," from BETWEEN ANGELS by Stephen Dunn. Copyright © 1989 by Stephen Dunn. Reprinted by permission of W. W. Norton & Company, Inc.

James A. Emanuel: "Get Up, Blues" from WHOLE GRAIN: COL-LECTED POEMS, 1958–1989 (Detroit: Lotus Press, 1991) by James A. Emanuel. Reprinted by permission of James A. Emanuel.

Robert Frost: "The Road Not Taken," "Acquainted with the Night," "Into My Own," "Escapist-Never" and "Stopping by the Woods on a Snowy Evening" from THE POETRY OF ROBERT FROST, edited by Edward Connery Lathem, Copyright 1944, 1951, 1956, 1962 by Robert Frost. © 1970 by Lesley Frost Ballentine. Copyright © 1916, 1928, 1934, 1969 by Henry Holt & Company. Reprinted by permission of Henry Holt & Co., Inc.

Langston Hughes: "The Negro Speaks of Rivers," "Pennsylvania Station," and "Death of an Old Seaman" from COLLECTED POEMS by Langston Hughes. Copyright © 1994 by the Estate of Langston Hughes. Reprinted by permission of Alfred A. Knopf, Inc.

Archibald MacLeish: "Seafarer," from COLLECTED POEMS 1917–1982 by Archibald MacLeish. Copyright © 1985 by The Estate of Archibald MacLeish. Reprinted by permission of Houghton Mifflin Company. All rights reserved.

Claude McKay: "The Tropics in New York" from SELECTED POEMS OF CLAUDE MCKAY, Twayne Publishers, Inc.

Ogden Nash: "Riding on a Railroad Train," from I WOULDN'T HAVE MISSED IT by Ogden Nash. Copyright © 1935 by Ogden Nash. First appeared in THE SATURDAY EVENING POST. By permission of Little, Brown and Company.

Theodore Roethke: "Night Journey" from THE COLLECTED POEMS OF THEODORE ROETHKE (1940) reprinted by permission of Doubleday, a division of Bantam Doubleday Dell Publishing Group, Inc.

Mark Van Doren: "A Dream of Trains" from GOOD MORNING: LAST POEMS by Mark Van Doren. Copyright © 1973 by The Estate of Mark Van Doren. Reprinted by permission of Hill and Wang, a division of Farrar, Straus & Giroux, Inc.

Gene Zeiger: "Highway" reprinted by permission of Gene Zeiger. Previously published in *Drive, They Said: Poems about Americans and Their Cars* (Milkweed Editions, 1994), edited by Kurt Brown.

Contents

SEA, RAIL AND SKY

HOME, REST AND FINAL VOYAGES

SONGS FOR THE OPEN ROAD

From Song of the Open Road

Afoot and light-hearted I take to the open road,
Healthy, free, the world before me,
The long brown path before me leading me wherever I choose.

Henceforth I ask not good-fortune, I myself am good-fortune.
Henceforth I whimper no more, postpone no more, need nothing,
Done with indoor complaints, libraries, querulous criticisms,
Strong and content I travel the open road.

Walt Whitman

There Is No Frigate Like a Book

There is no frigate like a book
    To take us lands away,
Nor any coursers like a page
    Of prancing poetry.
This traverse may the poorest take
    Without oppress of toll;
How frugal is the chariot
    That bears a human soul!

Emily Dickinson

From Childe Harold's Pilgrimage

There is a pleasure in the pathless woods,
    There is a rapture on the lonely shore,
There is society where none intrudes,

1

By the deep sea, and music in its roar.
I love not man the less, but Nature more,
From these our interviews, in which I steal
    From all I may be, or have been before,
To mingle with the universe, and feel
What I can ne'er express, yet can not all conceal.

George Gordon, Lord Byron

The Vagabond

Give to me the life I love,
    Let the lave go by me,
Give the jolly heaven above
    And the byway nigh me.
Bed in the bush with stars to see,
    Bread I dip in the river—
There's the life for a man like me,
    There's the life forever.

Let the blow fall soon or late,
    Let what will be o'er me;
Give the face of earth around
    And the road before me.
Wealth I seek not, hope nor love,
    Nor a friend to know me;
All I seek, the heaven above
    And the road below me.

Or let autumn fall on me
    Where afield I linger,
Silencing the bird on tree,
    Biting the blue finger,
White as meal the frosty field—
    Warm the fireside haven—
Not to autumn will I yield,
    Nor to winter even!

Let the blow fall soon or late,
    Let what will be o'er me;
Give the face of earth around,
    And the road before me.
Wealth I ask not, hope nor love,
    Nor a friend to know me;

All I ask the heaven above,
And the road below me.

Robert Louis Stevenson

Ithaka

When you set out for Ithaka
ask that your way be long,
full of adventure, full of instruction.
The Laistrygonians and the Cyclops,
angry Poseidon—do not fear them:
such as these you will never find
as long as your thought is lofty, as long as a rare
emotion touch your spirit and your body.
The Laistrygonians and the Cyclops,
wild Poseidon—you will not meet them
unless you carry them in your soul,
unless your soul raises them up before you.

Ask that your way be long.
At many a summer dawn to enter
—with what gratitude, what joy—
ports seen for the first time;
to stop at Phoenician trading centres
and to buy good merchandise,
mother of pearl and coral, amber and ebony,
sensuous perfumes of every kind,
sensuous perfumes as lavishly as you can;
to visit many Egyptian cities,
to gather stores of knowledge from the learned.

Have Ithaka always in your mind.
Your arrival there is what you are destined for.
But do not in the least hurry the journey.
Better that it lasts for years,
so that when you reach the island you are old,
rich with all you have gained on the way,
not expecting Ithaka to give you wealth.

Ithaka gave you the splendid journey.
Without her you would not have set out.
She hasn't anything else to give you.

And if you find her poor, Ithaka has not deceived you.
So wise have you become, of such experience,
that already you will have understood what these Ithakas mean.

> Constantine Cavafy
> (translated by Edmund Keeley and Philip Sherrard)

Song of Songs

My beloved spake, and said unto me,
Rise up, my love, my fair one and come away.
For, lo, the winter is past,
the rain is over and gone;
the flowers appear on the earth;
the time of the singing of birds is come,
and the voice of the turtle is heard in our land;
the fig tree putteth forth her green figs,
and the vines with the tender grape give a good smell.
Arise, my love, my fair one, and come away.

> The Song of Solomon, 2:10-13
> King James Bible

what is

what is
a
voyage
?

up
upup:go
ing

downdowndown

com;ing won
der
ful sun

moon stars the all,& a

(big
ger than
big

gest could even

begin to be)dream
of;a thing;of
a creature who's

O

cean
(everywhere
nothing

but light and dark;but

never forever
& when)un
til one strict

here of amazing most

now, with what
thousands of(hundreds
of)millions of

CriesWhichAreWings

E. E. Cummings

somewhere i have never travelled,gladly beyond

somewhere i have never travelled,gladly beyond
any experience,your eyes have their silence:
in your most frail gesture are things which enclose me,
or which i cannot touch because they are too near

your slightest look easily will unclose me
though I have closed myself as fingers,
you open myself as fingers,
you open always petal by petal myself as Spring opens
(touching skillfully,mysteriously)her first rose

or if you wish be to close me,i and
my life will shut very beautifully,suddenly,
as when the heart of this flower imagines
the snow carefully everywhere descending;

nothing which we are to perceive in this world equals
the power of your intense fragility:whose texture

compels me with the colour of its countries,
rendering death and forever with each breathing

(i do not know what it is about you that closes
and opens; only something in me understands
the voice of your eyes is deeper than all roses)
nobody,not even the rain,has such small hands

E. E. Cummings

On First Looking into Chapman's Homer

Much have I traveled in the realms of gold,
    And many goodly states and kingdoms seen;
    Round many western islands have I been
Which bards in fealty to Apollo hold.
Oft of one wide expanse had I been told
    That deep-browed Homer ruled as his demesne,
    Yet did I never breathe its pure serene
Till I heard Chapman speak out loud and bold.
Then felt I like some watcher of the skies
    When a new planet swims into his ken;
Or like stout Cortez when with eagle eyes
    He stared at the Pacific—and all his men
Looked at each other with a wild surmise—
    Silent, upon a peak in Darien.

John Keats

On Journeys Through the States

On journeys through the States we start,
(Ay through the world, urged by these songs,
Sailing henceforth to every land, to every sea,)
We willing learners of all, teachers of all, and lovers of all.

We have watch'd the seasons dispensing themselves and passing one,
And have said, Why should not a man or woman do as much as the
    seasons, and effuse as much?

We dwell a while in every city and town,
We pass through Kanada, the North-east, the vast valley of the
    Mississippi, and the Southern States,
We confer on equal terms with each of the States,

We make trial of ourselves and invite men and women to hear,
We say to ourselves, Remember, fear not, be candid, promulge the
    body and the soul,
Dwell a while and pass on, be copious, temperate, chaste, magnetic,
And what you effuse may then return as the seasons return,
And may be just as much as the seasons.

Walt Whitman

Recuerdo

We were very tired, we were very merry—
We had gone back and forth all night on the ferry.
It was bare and bright, and smelled like a table,
We lay on a hilltop underneath the moon;
And the whistles kept blowing, and the dawn came soon.

We were very tired, we were very merry—
We had gone back and forth all night on the ferry;
And you ate an apple, and I ate a pear,
From a dozen of each we had bought somewhere;
And the sky went wan, and the wind came cold,
And the sun rose dripping, a bucketful of gold.

We were very tired, we were very merry,
We had gone back and forth all night on the ferry.
We hailed, "Good morrow, mother!" to a shawl-covered head,
And bought a morning paper, which neither of us read;
And she wept, "God bless you!" for the apples and pears,
And we gave her all our money but our subway fares.

Edna St. Vincent Millay

A Vagabond Song

There is something in the autumn that is native to my blood—
Touch of manner, hint of mood;
And my heart is like a rhyme,
With the yellow and the purple and the crimson keeping time.

The scarlet of the maples can shake me like a cry
Of bugles going by.
And my lonely spirit thrills
To see the frosty asters like a smoke upon the hills.

There is something in October sets the gypsy blood astir;
We must rise and follow here,
When from every hill of flame
She calls and calls each vagabond by name.

Bliss Carman

From **A Rolling Stone**

To pitch my tent with no prosy plan,
    To range and to change at will;
To mock at the mastership of man,
    To see Adventure's thrill.
Carefree to be, as a bird that sings;
    To go my own sweet way;
To reck not at all what may befall,
    But to live and to love each day.

To scorn all strife, and to view all life
    With the curious eyes of a child;
From the plangent sea of the prairie,
    From the slum to the heart of the Wild.
From the red-rimmed star to the speck of sand,
    From the vast to the greatly small;
For I know that the whole for good is planned,
    And I want to see it all.

Robert Service

The Land of Beyond

Have ever you heard of the Land of Beyond
    That dreams at the gates of the day?
Alluring it lies at the skirts of the skies,
    And ever so far away;
Alluring it calls: O ye the yoke galls,
    And ye of the trail overfond,
With saddle and pack, by paddle and track,
    Let's go to the Land of Beyond!

Have ever you stood where the silences brood,
    And vast the horizons begin,
At the dawn of the day to behold far away
    The goal you would strive for and win?

Yet ah! in the night when you gain to the height,
    With the vast pool of heaven star-spawned,
Afar and agleam, like a valley of dream,
    Still mocks you a Land of Beyond.

Thank God! there is always a Land of Beyond
    For us who are true to the trail;
A vision to seek, a beckoning peak,
    A farness that never will fail;
A pride in our soul that mocks at a goal,
    A manhood that irks at a bond,
And try how we will, unattainable still,
    Behold it, our Land of Beyond!

Robert Service

On the World

The world's an inn; and I her guest.
I eat; I drink; I take my rest.
My hostess, nature, does deny me
Nothing, wherewith she can supply me;
Where, having stayed a while, I pay
Her lavish bills, and go my way.

Francis Quarles

"Great things are done when men & mountains meet"

Great things are done when Men & Mountains meet
This is not Done by Jostling in the Street

William Blake

Roadways

One road leads to London,
    One road runs to Wales,
My road leads me seawards
    To the white dipping sails.

One road leads to the river,
    As it goes singing slow;
My road leads to shipping,
    Where the bronzed sailors go.

Leads me, lures me, calls me
    To salt green tossing sea;
A road without earth's road-dust
    Is the right road for me.

A wet road heaving, shining,
    And wild with seagull's cries,
A mad salt sea-wind blowing
    The salt spray in my eyes.

My road calls me, lures me
    West, east, south, and north;
Most roads lead men homewards,
    My road leads me forth

To add more miles to the tally
    Of grey miles left behind,
In quest of that one beauty
    God put me here to find.

                        John Masefield

Out Where the West Begins

Out where the handclasp's a little stronger,
Out where the smile dwells a little longer,
    That's where the West begins;
Out where the sun is a little brighter,
Where the snows that fall are a trifle whiter,
Where the bonds of home are a wee bit tighter,—
    That's where the West begins.

Out where the skies are a trifle bluer,
Out where friendship's a little truer,
    That's where the West begins;
Out where a fresher breeze is blowing,
Where there's laughter in every streamlet flowing,
Where there's more of reaping and less of sowing,—
    That's where the West begins.

Out where the world is in the making,
Where fewer hearts in despair are aching,
    That's where the West begins;

Where there's more of singing and less of sighing,
Where there's more of giving and less of buying,
And a man makes friends without half trying—
　　That's where the West begins.

                                        Arthur Chapman

Highway

Glow of ice on the dark maples,
shape of a blue fish in the clouds,
hum of tires, stutter of the car radio.
You know the highway is kindly,
the curve of it, your family at the end of it,
the lull of the wheels, the sudden view
of a mill town dropped among trees
thin as eyelashes, and the buildings,
small heaving chests with breaths
of smoke. And a sudden tenderness
fills you for the idea of people,
their wills and habits, the machinery
of their kindness, the way meals are
served with salt and with a spoon.
And you think of them as birds
driven by some wind, and such mercy
passes that it makes you weep for it
and soon you can't see the road
for the awful kindness of it, and
the idea of *you*, your name vanishes
leaving you so alone that you must reclaim
it fast as you can in thought,
that dark bird circling over
the road until you are lost, or found
again in its wide wings lacing the blue
moving sky, the car now in motion
past the flash of sun again on an icy branch,
the self safely wrapped back inside its body,
which is your own, driving a car, yours.

                                        Gene Zeiger

The Sacred

After the teacher asked if anyone had
     a sacred place
and the students fidgeted and shrank

in their chairs, the most serious of them all
     said it was his car,
being in it alone, his tape deck playing

things he'd chosen, and others knew the truth
     had been spoken
and began speaking about their rooms,

their hiding places, but the car kept coming up,
     the car in motion,
music filling it, and sometimes one other person

who understood the bright altar of the dashboard
     and how far away
a car could take him from the need

to speak, or to answer, the key
     in having a key
and putting it in, and going.

                               Stephen Dunn

The Lake Isle of Innisfree

I will arise and go now, and go to Innisfree,
And a small cabin build there, of clay and wattles made:
Nine bean-rows will I have there, a hive for the honey-bee,
And live alone in the bee-loud glade.

And I shall have some peace there, for peace comes dropping slow,
Dropping from the veils of the morning to where the cricket sings;
There midnight's all a glimmer, and noon a purple glow,
And evening full of the linnet's wings.

I will arise and go now, for always night and day
I hear lake water lapping with low sounds by the shore;
While I stand on the roadway, or on the pavements gray,
I hear it in the deep heart's core.

                           William Butler Yeats

I Was Born Upon Thy Bank, River

I was born upon thy bank, river,
   My blood flows in thy stream,
And thou meanderest forever
   At the bottom of my dream.

                    Henry David Thoreau

The Road Not Taken

Two roads diverged in a yellow wood,
And sorry I could not travel both
And be one traveler, long I stood
And looked down one as far as I could
To where it bent in the undergrowth;

Then took the other, as just as fair,
And having perhaps the better claim,
Because it was grassy and wanted wear;
Though as for that the passing there
Had worn them really about the same,

And both that morning equally lay
In leaves no step had trodden black.
Oh, I kept the first for another day!
But knowing how way leads on to way,
I doubted if I should ever come back.

I shall be telling this with a sigh
Somewhere ages and ages hence:
Two roads diverged in a wood, and I—
I took the one less traveled by,
And that has made all the difference.

                    Robert Frost

Stopping by Woods on a Snowy Evening

Whose woods these are I think I know.
His house is in the village, though;
He will not see me stopping here
To watch his woods fill up with snow.

My little horse must think it queer
To stop without a farmhouse near
Between the woods and frozen lake
The darkest evening of the year.

He gives his harness bells a shake
To ask if there is some mistake.
The only other sound's the sweep
Of easy wind and downy flake.

The woods are lovely, dark and deep.
But I have promises to keep,
And miles to go before I sleep,
And miles to go before I sleep.

Robert Frost

Acquainted with the Night

I have been one acquainted with the night.
I have walked out in rain—and back in rain.
I have outwalked the furthest city light.

I have looked down the saddest city lane.
I have passed by the watchman on his beat
And dropped my eyes, unwilling to explain.

I have stood still and stopped the sound of feet
When far away an interrupted cry
Came over houses from another street,

But not to call me back or say good-by;
And further still at an unearthly height
One luminary clock against the sky

Proclaimed the time was neither wrong nor right.
I have been one acquainted with the night.

Robert Frost

When I Heard the Learn'd Astronomer

When I heard the learn'd astronomer,
When the proofs, the figures, were ranged in columns before me,
When I was shown the charts and diagrams, to add, divide, and mea-
sure them,

When I sitting heard the astronomer where he lectured with much
      applause in the lecture-room,
How soon unaccountable I became tired and sick,
Till rising and gliding out I wander'd off by myself,
In the mystical moist night-air, and from time to time,
Look'd up in perfect silence at the stars.

                        Walt Whitman

The Negro Speaks of Rivers
To W.E.B. Du Bois

I've known rivers:
I've known rivers ancient as the world and older than the flow of
      human blood in human veins.

My soul has grown deep like the rivers.

I bathed in the Euphrates when dawns were young.
I built my hut near the Congo and it lulled me to sleep.
I looked upon the Nile and raised the pyramids above it.
I heard the singing of the Mississippi when Abe Lincoln went down
      to New Orleans, and I've seen its muddy bosom turn all golden
      in the sunset.

I've known rivers:
Ancient, dusky rivers.

My soul has grown deep like the rivers.

                    Langston Hughes

The Stolen Child

Where dips the rocky highland
Of Sleuth Wood in the lake,
There lies a leafy island
Where flapping herons wake
The drowsy water-rats;
There we've hid our faery vats,
Full of berries,
And of reddest stolen cherries.
    Come away, O human child!
    To the waters and the wild
    With a faery, hand in hand,
    For the world's more full of weeping than you can understand.

Where the wave of moonlight glosses
The dim gray sands with light,
Far off by furthest Rosses
We foot it all the night,
Weaving olden dances,
Mingling hands and mingling glances
Till the moon has taken flight;
To and fro we leap
And chase the frothy bubbles,
While the world is full of troubles
And is anxious in its sleep.
> *Come away, O human child!*
> *To the waters and the wild*
> *With a faery, hand in hand,*
> *For the world's more full of weeping than you can understand.*

Where the wandering water gushes
From the hills above Glen-Car,
In pools among the rushes
That scarce could bathe a star,
We seek for slumbering trout
And whispering in their ears
Give them unquiet dreams;
Leaning softly out
From ferns that drop their tears
Over the young streams.
> *Come away, O human child!*
> *To the waters and the wild*
> *With a faery, hand in hand,*
> *For the world's more full of weeping than you can understand.*

Away with us he's going,
The solemn-eyed:
He'll hear no more the lowing
Of the calves on the warm hillside;
Or the kettle on the hob
Sing peace into his breast,
Or see the brown mice bob
Round and round the oatmeal-chest.
> *For he comes, the human child,*
> *To the waters and the wild*
> *With a faery, hand in hand,*
> *From a world more full of weeping than he can understand.*

William Butler Yeats

Sonnet—to an American Painter Departing for Europe

Thine eyes shall see the light of distant skies:
>   Yet, Cole! thy heart shall bear to Europe's strand
>   A living image of thy native land,
Such as on thy own glorious canvass lies.
Lone lakes—savannahs where the bison roves—
>   Rocks rich with summer garlands—solemn streams—
>   Skies, where the desert eagle wheels and screams—
Spring bloom and autumn blaze of boundless groves.
Fair scenes shall greet thee where thou goest—fair,
>   But different—every where the trace of men,
>   Paths, homes, graves, ruins, from the lowest glen
To where life shrinks from the fierce Alpine air.
>   Gaze on them, till the tears shall dim thy sight,
>   But keep that earlier, wilder image bright.

William Cullen Bryant

Into My Own

One of my wishes is that those dark trees,
So old and firm they scarcely hold the breeze,
Were not, as 'twere, the merest mask of gloom,
But stretched away unto the edge of doom.

I should not be withheld but that some day
Into their vastness I should steal away,
Fearless of ever finding open land,
Or highway where the slow wheel pours the sand.

I do not see why I should e'er turn back
Or those should not set forth upon my track
To overtake me, who should miss me here
And long to know if still I held them dear.

They would not find me changed from him they knew—
Only more sure of all I thought was true.

Robert Frost

Escapist—Never

He is no fugitive—escaped, escaping.
No one has seen him stumble looking back.
His fear is not behind him but beside him
On either hand to make his course perhaps
A crooked straightness yet no less a straightness.
He runs face forward. He is a pursuer.
He seeks a seeker who in his turn seeks
Another still, lost far into the distance.
Any who seek him seek in him the seeker.
His life is a pursuit of a pursuit forever.
It is the future that creates his present.
All is an interminable chain of longing.

Robert Frost

To the Not Impossible Him

How shall I know, unless I go
   To Cairo and Cathay,
Whether or not this blessed spot
   Is blest in every way?

Now it may be, the flower for me
   Is this beneath my nose;
How shall I tell, unless I smell
   The Carthaginian rose?

The fabric of my faithful love
   No power shall dim or ravel
Whilst I stay here,—but oh, my dear,
   If I should ever travel!

Edna St. Vincent Millay

SEA, RAIL AND SKY

From Childe Harold's Pilgrimage

Adieu, adieu! my native shore
        Fades o'er the waters blue;
The night-winds sigh, the breakers roar,
        And shrieks the wild sea-mew.
Yon sun that sets upon the sea
        We follow in his flight;
Farewell awhile to him and thee,
        My native Land—Good Night!

A few short hours, and he will rise
        To give the morrow birth;
And I shall hail the main and skies,
        But not my mother earth.
Deserted is my own good hall,
        Its hearth is desolate;
Wild weeds are gathering on the wall;
        My dog howls at the gate.

                George Gordon, Lord Byron

Sea-Fever

I must go down to the seas again, to the lonely sea and the sky,
And all I ask is a tall ship and a star to steer her by,
And the wheel's kick and the wind's song and the white sail's shaking,
And a grey mist on the sea's face and a grey dawn breaking.

I must go down to the seas again, for the call of the running tide
Is a wild call and a clear call that may not be denied;
And all I ask is a windy day with the white clouds flying,
And the flung spray and the blown spume, and the seagulls crying.

I must go down to the seas again to the vagrant gypsy life,
To the gull's way and the whale's way where the wind's like a whetted
    knife;
And all I ask is a merry yarn from a laughing fellow-rover,
And quiet sleep and a sweet dream when the long trick's over.

                                            John Masefield

Exultation is in the Going

Exultation is in the going
Of an inland soul to sea,
Past the houses—past the headlands—
Into deep Eternity—

Bred as we, among the mountains,
Can the sailor understand
The divine intoxication
Of the first league out from land?

                                            Emily Dickinson

The Secret of the Sea

Ah! what pleasant visions haunt me
    As I gaze upon the sea!
All the old romantic legends,
    All my dreams, come back to me.

Sails of silk and ropes of sandal,
    Such as gleam in ancient lore;
And the singing of the sailors,
    And the answer from the shore!

Most of all, the Spanish ballad
    Haunts me oft, and tarries long,
Oft the noble Count Arnaldos
    And the sailor's mystic song.

Like the long waves on a sea-bench,
  Where the sand as silver shines,
With a soft, monotonous cadence,
  Flow its unrhymed lyric lines;—

Telling how the Count Arnaldos,
  With his hawk upon his hand,
Saw a fair and stately galley,
  Steering onward to the land;—

How he heard the ancient helmsman
  Chant a song so wild and clear,
That the sailing sea-bird slowly
  Poised upon the mast to hear,

Till his soul was full of longing,
  And he cried, with impulse strong,—
"Helmsman! for the love of heaven,
  Teach me, too, that wondrous song!"

"Wouldst thou,"—so the helmsman answered,
  "Learn the secret of the sea?
Only those who brave its dangers
  Comprehend its mystery!"

In each sail that skims the horizon,
  In each landward-blowing breeze,
I behold that stately galley,
  Hear those mournful melodies;

Till my soul is full of longing
  For the secret of the sea,
And the heart of the great ocean
  Sends a thrilling pulse through me.

Henry Wadsworth Longfellow

Put Off Thy Bark from Shore, Though Near the Night

Put off thy bark from shore, though near the night,
And leaving home and friends and hope behind,
Sail down the lights. Thou scarce canst fail to find,
O desolate one, the morning breaking white,
Some shore of rest beyond the laboring wave.

Ah, 'tis for this I mourn: too long I have
Wandered in tears along life's stormy way
Where day to day no haven or hope reveals.
Yet on the bound my weary sight I keep
As one who sails, a landsman on the deep,
And longing for the land, day after day
Sees the horizon rise and fall and feels
His heart die out, still riding restlessly
Between the sailing cloud and the seasick sea.

                              Frederick Goddard Tuckerman

Golden Moonrise

When your eyes gaze seaward
Piercing through the dim
Slow descending nightfall,
On the outer rim

Where the deep blue silence
Touches sky and sea,
Hast thou seen the golden
Moon, rise silently?

Seen the great battalions
Of the stars grow pale—
Melting in the magic
Of her silver veil?

I have seen the wonder,
I have felt the balm
Of the golden moonrise
Turn to silver calm.

                              William Stanley Braithwaite

Exiled

Searching my heart for its true sorrow,
        This is the thing I find to be:
That I am weary of words and people,
        Sick on the city, wanting the sea;

Wanting the sticky, salty sweetness
        Of the strong wind and shattered spray;

Wanting the loud sound and the soft sound
    Of the big surf that breaks all day.

Always before about my dooryard,
    Marking the reach of the winter sea,
Rooted in sand and dragging driftwood,
    Straggled the purple wild sweet pea;

Always I climbed the wave at morning,
    Shook the sand from my shoes at night,
That now am caught beneath great buildings,
    Stricken with noise, confused with light.

If I could hear the green piles groaning
    Under the windy wooden piers,
See again the bobbing barrels,
    And the black sticks that fence the weirs,

If I could see the weedy mussels
    Crusting the wrecked and rotting hulls,
Hear once again the hungry crying
    Overhead, of the wheeling gulls,

Feel once again the shanty straining
    Under the turning of the tide
Fear once again the rising freshet,
    Dread the bell in the fog outside,

I should be happy—that was happy
    All day long on the coast of Maine.
I have a need to hold and handle
    Shells and anchors and ships again!

I should be happy, that am happy
    Never at all since I came here.
I am too long away from water.
    I have a need of water near.

                    Edna St. Vincent Millay

A Strip of Blue

I do not own an inch of land,
    But all I see is mine,—
The orchard and the mowing-fields,
    The lawns and gardens fine.

The winds my tax-collectors are,
    They bring me tithes divine,—
Wild scents and subtle essences,
    A tribute rare and free;
And, more magnificent than all,
    My window keeps for me
A glimpse of blue immensity,—
    A little strip of sea.

Richer am I than he who owns
    Great fleets and argosies;
I have a share in every ship
    Won by the inland breeze,
To loiter on yon airy road
    Above the apple-trees,
I freight them with my untold dreams;
    Each bears my own picked crew;
And nobler cargoes wait for them
    Than ever India knew,—
My ships that sail into the East
    Across that outlet blue.

Sometimes they seem like living shapes,—
    The people of the sky,—
Guests in white raiment coming down
    From heaven, which is close by;
I call them by familiar names,
    As one by one draws nigh,
So white, so light, so spirit-like,
    From violet mists they bloom!
The aching wastes of the unknown
    Are half reclaimed from gloom,
Since on life's hospitable sea
    All souls find sailing-room.

The ocean grows a weariness
    With nothing else in sight;
Its east and west, its north and south,
    Spread out from morn till night;
We miss the warm, caressing shore,
    Its brooding shade and light.

                                                Lucy Larcom

In Cabin'd Ships At Sea

In cabin'd ships at sea,
The boundless blue on every side expanding,
With whistling winds and music of the waves, the large imperious
    waves,
Or some lone bark buoy'd on the dense marine,
Where joyous full of faith, spreading white sails,
She cleaves the ether mid the sparkle and the foam of day, or under
    many a star at night,
By sailors young and old haply will I, a reminiscence of the land, be
    read,
In full rapport at last.

Here are our thoughts, voyagers' thoughts.
Here not the land, firm land, alone appears, may then by them be said,
The sky o'erarches here, we feel the undulating deck beneath our feet,
We feel the long pulsation, ebb and flow of endless motion,
The tones of unseen mystery, the vague and vast suggestions of the
    briny world, the liquid-flowing syllables,
The perfume, the faint creaking of the cordage, the melancholy rhythm,
The boundless vista and the horizon far and dim are all here.
And this is ocean's poem.

Then falter not O book, fulfil your destiny,
You not a reminiscence of the land alone,
You too as a lone bark cleaving the ether, purpos'd I know not
    whither, yet ever full of faith,
Consort to every ship that sails, sail you!
Bear forth to them folded my love, (dear mariners, for you I fold it
    here in every leaf;)
Speed on my book! spread your white sails my little bark athwart the
    imperious waves,
Chant on, sail on, bear o'er the boundless blue from me to every sea,
The song for mariners and all their ships.

                                   Walt Whitman

Columbus

    Behind him lay the gray Azores,
      Behind the Gates of Hercules;
    Before him not the ghost of shores,
      Before him only shoreless seas.

The good mate said: "Now must we pray,
   For lo! the very stars are gone.
Brave Admiral, speak, what shall I say?"
   "Why, say, 'Sail on! sail on! and on!'"

"My men grow mutinous day by day;
   My men grow ghastly wan and weak."
The stout mate thought of home; a spray
   Of salt wave washed his swarthy cheek.
"What shall I say, brave Admiral, say,
   If we sight naught but seas at dawn?"
"Why, you shall say at break of day,
   'Sail on! sail on! sail on! and on!'"

They sailed and sailed, as winds might blow,
   Until at last the blanched mate said:
"Why, now not even God would know
   Should I and all my men fall dead.
These very winds forget their way,
   For God from those dread seas is gone.
Now speak, brave Admiral, speak and say" —
   He said: "Sail on! sail on! and on!"

They sailed. They sailed. Then spake the mate:
   "This mad sea shows his teeth tonight.
He curls his lip, he lies in wait,
   With lifted teeth, as if to bite!
Brave Admiral, say but one good word:
   What shall we do when hope is gone?"
The words leapt like a leaping sword:
   "Sail on! sail on! sail on! and on!"

Then, pale and worn, he kept his deck,
   And peered through darkness. Ah, that night
Of all dark nights! And then a speck —
   A light! A light! A light! A light!
It grew, a starlit flag unfurled!
   It grew to be Time's burst of dawn.
He gained a world; he gave that world
   Its grandest lesson: "On! sail on!"

                          Joaquin Miller

Song

The boat is chafing at our long delay,
  And we must leave too soon
The spicy sea-pinks and the inborne spray,
  The tawny sands, the moon.

Keep us, O Thetis, in our western flight!
  Watch from thy pearly throne
Our vessel, plunging deeper into night
  To reach a land unknown.

                              John Davidson

The Winds of Fate

One ship drives east and another drives west
    With the selfsame winds that blow.
        'Tis the set of the sails
        And not of the gales
    Which tells us the way to go.

Like the winds of the sea are the ways of fate,
    As we voyage along through life;
        'Tis the set of a soul
        That decides its goal,
    And not the calm or the strife.

                            Ella Wheeler Wilcox

Seafarer

And learn O voyager to walk
The roll of earth, the pitch and fall
That swings across these trees those stars:
That swings the sunlight up the wall.

And learn upon these narrow beds
To sleep in spite of sea, in spite
Of sound the rushing planet makes:
And learn to sleep against this ground.

                            Archibald MacLeish

All Day I Hear the Noise of Waters

All day I hear the noise of waters
     Making moan,
Sad as the sea-bird is, when going
     Forth alone,
He hears the winds cry to the waters'
     Monotone.

The grey winds, the cold winds are blowing
     Where I go.
I hear the noise of many waters
     Far below.
All day, all night, I hear them flowing
     To and fro.

          James Joyce

The Tide Rises, the Tide Falls

The tide rises, the tide falls,
The twilight darkens, the curlew calls;
Along the sea-sands damp and brown
The traveller hastens toward the town,
     And the tide rises, the tide falls.

Darkness settles on roofs and walls,
But the sea, the sea in the darkness calls;
The little waves, with their soft, white hands,
Efface the footprints in the sands,
     And the tide rises, the tide falls.

The morning breaks; the steeds in their stalls
Stamp and neigh, as the hostler calls;
The day returns, but nevermore
Returns the traveller to the shore,
     And the tide rises, the tide falls.

          Henry Wadsworth Longfellow

From the Shore

A lone gray bird,
Dim-dipping, far-flying,
Alone in the shadows and grandeurs and tumults

Of night and the sea
And the stars and storms.
Out over the darkness it wavers and hovers,
Out into the gloom it swings and batters,
Out into the wind and the rain and the vast,
Out into the pit of a great black world,
Where fogs are at battle, sky-driven, sea-blown,
Love of mist and rapture of flight,
Glories of chance and hazards of death
On its eager and palpitant wings.
Out into the deep of the great dark world,
Beyond the long borders where foam and drift
Of the sundering waves are lost and gone
On the tides that plunge and rear and crumble.

Carl Sandburg

Impressions

I
Les Silhouettes

The sea is flecked with bars of grey,
The dull dead wind is out of tune,
And like a withered leaf the moon
Is blown across the stormy bay.

Etched clear upon the pallid sand
The black boat lies: a sailor boy
Clambers aboard in careless joy
With laughing face and gleaming hand.

And overhead the curlews cry,
Where through the dusky upland grass
The young brown-throated reapers pass,
Like silhouettes against the sky.

Oscar Wilde

The Flying Dutchman

Unyielding in the pride of his defiance,
  Afloat with none to serve or to command,
Lord of himself at last, and all by Science,
  He seeks the Vanished Land.

Alone, by the one light of his one thought,
    He steers to find the shore from which we came,
Fearless of in what coil he may be caught
    On seas that have no name.

Into the night he sails; and after night
    There is a dawning, though there be no sun;
Wherefore, with nothing but himself in sight,
    Unsighted, he sails on.

At last there is a lifting of the cloud
    Between the flood before him and the sky;
And then—though he may curse the Power aloud
    That has no power to die—

He steers himself away from what is haunted
    By the old ghost of what has been before,—
Abandoning, as always, and undaunted,
    One fog-walled island more.

Edwin Arlington Robinson

Ships That Pass in the Night

Out in the sky the great dark clouds are massing;
    I look far out into the pregnant night,
Where I can hear a solemn booming gun
    And catch the gleaming of a random light,
That tells me that the ship I seek is passing, passing.

My tearful eyes my soul's deep hurt are glassing;
    For I would hail and check that ship of ships.
I stretch my hands imploring, cry aloud,
    My voice falls dead a foot from mine own lips,
And but its ghost doth reach that vessel, passing, passing.

O Earth, O Sky, O Ocean, both surpassing,
    O heart of mine, O soul that dreads the dark!
Is there no hope for me? Is there no way
    That I may sight and check that speeding bark
Which out of sight and sound is passing, passing?

Paul Laurence Dunbar

From **My Lost Youth**

Often I think of the beautiful town
  That is sealed by the sea;
Often in thought go up and down
The pleasant streets of that dear old town,
  And my youth comes back to me.
    And a verse of a Lapland song
    Is haunting my memory still:
    "A boy's will is the wind's will,
And the thoughts of youth are long, long thoughts."

•••

Strange to me now are the forms I meet
  When I visit the dear old town;
But the native air is pure and sweet,
And the trees that o'ershadow each well-known street,
  As they balance up and down,
    Are singing the beautiful song,
    Are sighing and whispering still:
    "A boy's will is the wind's will,
And the thoughts of youth are long, long thoughts."

And Deering's Woods are fresh and fair,
  And with joy that is almost pain
My heart goes back to wander there,
And among the dreams of the days that were,
  I find my lost youth again.
    And the strange and beautiful song,
    The groves are repeating it still:
    "A boy's will is the wind's will,
And the thoughts of youth are long, long thoughts."

                    Henry Wadsworth Longfellow

Emigravit

With sails full set, the ship her anchor weighs.
Strange names shine out beneath her figure head.
What glad farewells with eager eyes are said!
What cheer for him who goes, and him who stays!

Fair skies, rich lands, new homes, and untried days
Some go to seek: the rest but wait instead,
Watching the way wherein their comrades led,
Until the next stanch ship her flag doth raise.
Who knows what myriad colonies there are
Of fairest fields, and rich, undreamed-of gains
Thick planted in the distant shining plains
Which we call sky because they lie so far?
Oh, write of me, not "Died in bitter pains,"
But "Emigrated to another star!"

Helen Hunt Jackson

Possibilities

Where are the poets, unto whom belong
    The Olympian heights; whose singing shafts were sent
    Straight to the mark, and not from bows half bent,
    But with the utmost tension of the thong?
Where are the stately argosies of song,
    Whose rushing keels made music as they went
    Sailing in search of some new continent,
    With all sail set, and steady winds and strong?
Perhaps there lives some dreamy boy, untaught
    In schools, some graduate of the field or street,
An admiral sailing the high seas of thought,
    Fearless and first, and steering with his fleet
    For lands not yet laid down in any chart.

Henry Wadsworth Longfellow

Song

Summer is over upon the sea.
The pleasure yacht, the social being,
that danced on the endless polished floor,
stepped and side-stepped like Fred Astaire,
is gone, is gone, docked somewhere ashore.

The friends have left, the sea is bare
that was strewn with floating, fresh green weeds.
Only the rusty-sided freighters

go past the moon's marketless craters
and the stars are the only ships of pleasure.

Elizabeth Bishop

Death of an Old Seaman

We buried him high on a windy hill,
But his soul went out to sea.
I know, for I heard, when all was still,
His sea-soul say to me:

Put no tombstone at my head,
For here I do not make my bed.
Strew no flowers on my grave,
I've gone back to the wind and wave.
Do not, do not weep for me,
For I am happy with my sea.

Langston Hughes

Ulysses

It little profits that an idle king,
By this still hearth, among these barren crags,
Matched with an aged wife, I mete and dole
Unequal laws unto a savage race
That hoard, and sleep, and feed, and know not me.
I cannot rest from travel; I will drink
Life to the lees. All times I have enjoyed
Greatly, have suffered greatly, both with those
That loved me, and alone; on shore, and when
Through scudding drifts the rainy Hyades
Vexed the dim sea. I am become a name;
For always roaming with a hungry heart
Much have I seen and known—cities of men
And manners, climates, councils, governments,
Myself not least, but honored of them all—
And drunk delight of battle with my peers,
Far on the ringing plains of windy Troy.
I am a part of all that I have met;
Yet all experience is an arch wherethrough

Gleams that untraveled world whose margin fades
Forever and forever when I move.
How dull it is to pause, to make an end,
To rust unburnished, not to shine in use!
As though to breathe were life! Life piled on life
Were all too little, and of one to me
Little remains; but every hour is saved
From that eternal silence, something more,
A bringer of new things; and vile it were
For some three suns to store and hoard myself,
And this gray spirit yearning in desire
To follow knowledge like a sinking star,
Beyond the utmost bound of human thought.

   This is my son, mine own Telemachus,
To whom I leave the sceptre and the isle—
Well-loved of me, discerning to fulfill
This labor, by slow prudence to make mild
A rugged people, and through soft degrees
Subdue them to the useful and the good.
Most blameless is he, centered in the sphere
Of common duties, decent not to fail
In offices of tenderness, and pay
Meet adoration to my household gods,
When I am gone. He works his work, I mine.

   There lies the port; the vessel puffs her sail;
There gloom the dark, broad seas. My mariners,
Souls that have toiled, and wrought, and thought with me—
That ever with a frolic welcome took
The thunder and the sunshine, and opposed
Free hearts, free foreheads—you and I are old;
Old age hath yet his honor and his toil.
Death closes all; but something ere the end,
Some work of noble note, may yet be done,
Not unbecoming men that strove with Gods.
The lights begin to twinkle from the rocks;
The long day wanes, the slow moon climbs; the deep
Moans round with many voices. Come, my friends,
'Tis not too late to seek a newer world.
Push off, and sitting well in order smite
The sounding furrows; for my purpose holds
To sail beyond the sunset, and the baths
Of all the western stars, until I die.
It may be that the gulfs will wash us down;
It may be we shall touch the Happy Isles,

And see the great Achilles, whom we knew.
Though much is taken, much abides; and though
We are not now that strength which in old days
Moved earth and heaven, that which we are, we are—
One equal temper of heroic hearts,
Made weak by time and fate, but strong in will
To strive, to seek, to find, and not to yield.

Alfred, Lord Tennyson

Travel

The railroad track is miles away,
    And the day is loud with voices speaking,
Yet there isn't a train goes by all day
    But I hear its whistle shrieking.

All night there isn't a train goes by,
    Though the night is still for sleep and dreaming,
But I see its cinders red on the sky,
    And hear its engines steaming.

My heart is warm with the friends I make,
    And better friends I'll not be knowing,
Yet there isn't a train I wouldn't take,
    No matter where it's going.

Edna St. Vincent Millay

I like to see it lap the Miles

I like to see it lap the miles,
And lick the valleys up,
And stop to feed itself at tanks;
And then, prodigious, step

Around a pile of mountains,
And, supercilious, peer
In shanties by the sides of roads;
And then a quarry pare

To fit its sides, and crawl between,
Complaining all the while
In horrid, hooting stanza;
Then chase itself down hill

And neigh like Boanerges;
Then, punctual as a star,
Stop—docile and omnipotent—
At its own stable door.

                                        Emily Dickinson

Riding on a Railroad Train

Some people like to hitch and hike;
They are fond of highway travel;
Their nostrils toil through gas and oil.
They choke on dust and gravel.
Unless they stop for the traffic cop
Their road is a fine-or-jail road,
But wise old I go rocketing by;
I'm riding on the railroad.

I love to loll like a limp rag doll
In a peripatetic salon;
To think and think of a long cool drink
And cry to the porter, *Allons!*
Now the clickety clack of wheel on track
Grows clickety clackety clicker:
The line is clear for the engineer
And it mounts to his head like liquor.

With a farewell scream of escaping steam
The boiler bows to the Diesel;
The Iron Horse has run its course
And we ride a chromium weasel;
We draw our power from the harnessed shower,
The lightning without the thunder,
But a train is a train and will so remain
While the rails glide glistening under.

Oh, some like trips in luxury ships,
And some in gasoline wagons,
And others swear by the upper air
And the wings of flying dragons.
Let each make haste to indulge his taste,
Be it beer, champagne or cider;
My private joy, both man and boy,
Is being a railroad rider.

                                        Ogden Nash

Taking the Night-Train

A tremulous word, a lingering hand, the burning
   Of restless passion smoldering—so we part;
Ah, slowly from the dark the world is turning
   When midnight stars shine in a heavy heart.

The streets are lighted, and the myriad faces
   Move through the gaslight, and the homesick feet
Pass by me, homeless; sweet and close embraces
   Charm many a threshold—laughs and kisses sweet.

From great hotels the stranger throng is streaming,
   The hurrying wheels in many a street are loud;
Within the depot, in the gaslight gleaming,
   A glare of faces, stands the waiting crowd.

The whistle screams; the wheels are rumbling slowly,
   The path before us glides into the light:
Behind, the city sinks in silence wholly;
   The panting engine leaps into the night.

I seem to see each street a mystery growing,
   In mist of dreamland—vague, forgotten air:
Does no sweet soul, awakened, feel me going?
   Loves no dear heart, in dreams, to keep me there?

                          John James Piatt

Night Journey

Now as the train bears west,
Its rhythm rocks the earth,
And from my Pullman berth
I stare into the night
While the others take their rest.
Bridges of iron lace,
A suddenness of trees,
A lap of mountain mist
All cross my line of sight,
Then a bleak wasted place,
And a lake below my knees.
Full on my neck I feel
The straining at a curve;
My muscles move with steel,
I wake in every nerve.

I watch a beacon swing
From dark to blazing bright;
We thunder through ravines
And gullies washed with light.
Beyond the mountain pass
Mist deepens on the pane;
We rush into a rain
That rattles double glass.
Wheels shake the roadbed stone,
The pistons jerk and shove,
I stay up half the night
To see the land I love.

                                   Theodore Roethke

Window

Night from a railroad car window
Is a great, dark, soft thing
Broken across with slashes of light.

                                   Carl Sandburg

Pennsylvania Station

The Pennsylvania Station in New York
Is like some vast basilica of old
That towers above the terrors of the dark
As bulwark and protection to the soul.
Now people who are hurrying alone
And those who come in crowds from far away
Pass through this great concourse of steel and stone
To trains, or else from trains out into day.
And as in great basilicas of old
The search was ever for a dream of God,
So here the search is still within each soul
Some seed to find to root in earthly sod,
Some seed to find that sprouts a holy tree
To glorify the earth—and you—and me.

                                   Langston Hughes

The Engine

Into a gloom of the deep, dark night,
   With panting breath and a startled scream;
Swift as a bird in sudden flight
   Darts this creature of steel and steam.

Awful dangers are lurking nigh,
   Rocks and chasms are near the track,
But straight by the light of its great white eye
   It speeds through the shadows, dense and black.

Terrible thoughts and fierce desires
   Trouble its mad heart many an hour,
Where burn and smoulder the hidden fires,
   Coupled ever with might and power.

It hates, as a wild horse hates the rein,
   The narrow track by vale and hill;
And shrieks with a cry of startled pain,
   And longs to follow its own wild will.

                         Ella Wheeler Wilcox

Midnight on the Great Western

In the third-class sat the journeying boy,
     And the roof-lamp's oily flame
Played down on his listless form and face,
Bewrapt past knowing to what he was going,
     Or whence he came.

In the band of his hat the journeying boy
     Had a ticket stuck; and a string
Around his neck bore the key of his box,
That twinkled gleams of the lamp's sad beams
     Like a living thing.

What past can be yours, O journeying boy
     Towards a world unknown,
Who calmly, as if incurious quite
On all at stake, can undertake
     This plunge alone?

Knows your soul a sphere, O journeying boy
          Our rude realms far above,
Whence with spacious vision you mark and mete
This region of sin that you find you in
          But are not of?

Thomas Hardy

To a Locomotive in Winter

Thee for my recitative,
Thee in the driving storm even as now, the snow, the winter-day
     declining,
Thee in thy panoply, thy measur'd dual throbbing and thy beat
     convulsive,
Thy black cylindric body, golden brass and silvery steel,
Thy ponderous side-bars, parallel and connecting rods, gyrating,
     shuttling at thy sides,
Thy metrical, now swelling pant and roar, now tapering in the distance,
Thy great protruding head-light fix'd in front,
Thy long, pale, floating vapor-pennants, tinged with delicate purple,
The dense and murky clouds out-belching from thy smoke-stack,
Thy knitted frame, thy springs and valves, the tremulous twinkle of
     thy wheels,
Thy train of cars behind, obedient, merrily following,
Through gale or calm, now swift, now slack, yet steadily careering;
Type of the modern—emblem of motion and power—pulse of the
     continent,
For once come serve the Muse and merge in verse, even as here I see thee,
With storm and buffeting gusts of wind and falling snow,
By day thy warning ringing bell to sound its notes,
By night thy silent signal lamps to swing.

Fierce-throated beauty!
Roll through my chant with all thy lawless music, thy swinging lamps
     at night,
Thy madly-whistled laughter, echoing, rumbling like an earthquake,
     rousing all,
Law of thyself complete, thine own track firmly holding
(No sweetness debonair of tearful harp or glib piano thine,)
Thy trills of shrieks by rocks and hills return'd,
Launch'd o'er the prairies wide, across the lakes,
To the free skies unspent and glad and strong.

Walt Whitman

A Dream of Trains

As long ago they raced,
Last night they raced again;
I heard them inside me,
I felt the roll of the land.

I looked out of a window
And I was moving too;
The moon above Nebraska,
Lonely and cold.

Mourned for all of the autumns
I had forgotten this:
The low hills that tilted,
The barrenness, the vast.

I think I will remember now
Until the end of the world
How lordly were the straightaways,
How lyrical the curves.

Mark Van Doren

High Flight

Oh, I have slipped the surly bonds of earth,
And danced the skies on laughter-silvered wings;
Sunward I've climbed and joined the tumbling mirth
Of sun-split clouds—and done a hundred things
You have not dreamed of—wheeled and soared and swung
High in the sunlit silence. Hov'ring there
I've chased the shouting wind along and flung
My eager craft through footless halls of air.
Up, up the long delirious burning blue
I've topped the wind-swept heights with easy grace,
Where never lark, or even eagle, flew;
And, while with silent, lifting mind I've trod
The high untrespassed sanctity of space,
Put out my hand, and touched the face of God.

John Gillespie Magee, Jr.

First Flight

Here is the perfect vision: in the dawn,
In smudgy dusk I rise above the plain
Of the Persian desert, daubed with shadow still,
And instantly below me lies the hill,
That rubbish heap once called the City of Rhey,
Where Caliph Harun Al-Rashid was born.

Behind me Zoroaster's mountain rises:
White Demavend turns fire to unseen day.
Like an unravelling tape streams back the way
That leads into the kernel of all Asia.

The desert skims below.
Like caterpillar trails the camels go
Marked broadly by their stacks of camel thorn.
Those fretful eruptions are the hills of Persia;
Those striped brocades her bright precarious corn.
Now is the world, the planet where I was born,
Dwindled, reduced in this light blue of morn
To detail seen upon a gigantic scale.

Beyond the Bears the dark begins to fail,
Now comes the light weltering through Carls' Wain,
Now between stars the dawn begins to flow,
Washing around their points in spate of green.

Beside my hand the stars hang close, go out,
Spent candles. Now the moon most surely dies,
So haggard hangs she on the Persian peaks,
Who whitens misty on an English lawn.

Now in great spirals going
I drop to the Caspian Sea.

Onward to Colchis!
                Now is a peccant world
Seen at the purest angle of the vision:
In perfect, poetic state she lies.

                    Dorothy Wellesley, Duchess of Wellington

To a Waterfowl

Whither, 'midst falling dew,
　While glow the heavens with the last steps of day,
Far, through their rosy depths, dost thou pursue
　Thy solitary way?

Vainly the fowler's eye
　Might mark thy distant flight to do thee wrong,
As, darkly painted on the crimson sky,
　Thy figure floats along.

Seek'st thou the plashy brink
　Of weedy lake, or marge of river wide,
Or where the rocking billows rise and sink
　On the chafed ocean's side?

There is a Power whose care
　Teaches thy way along that pathless coast—
The desert and illimitable air—
　Lone wandering, but not lost.

All day thy wings have fanned,
　At that far height, the cold, thin atmosphere,
Yet stoop not weary, to the welcome land,
　Though the dark night is near.

And soon that toil shall end;
　Soon shalt thou find a summer home, and rest,
And scream among thy fellows; reeds shall bend,
　Soon, o'er thy sheltered nest.

Thou'rt gone! the abyss of heaven
　Hath swallowed up thy form; yet on my heart
Deeply hath sunk the lesson thou hast given,
　And shall not soon depart.

He who, from zone to zone,
　Guides through the boundless sky thy certain flight,
In the long way that I must tread alone
　Will lead my steps aright.

                              William Cullen Bryant

The Journey Is Everything

Montaigne believed the journey, in itself,
Was the idea. Yet from this moving plane
I look down on the dazzle of the world,

Conscious of his words but wondering
When, when shall I be here, at journey's end?
The journey, said Montaigne, *is everything*.

Two hours ago the setting out began
With words of love. It is too soon to be
In love with landscape, altering below—

The flight upriver and the dwindling hills—
As if I came for this, a traveler,
And every wisp of cloud were an obsession.

It is too soon! The journey is myself,
Concerned with where I was, where I must go,
Not with the clouds about me (what of them?),

Not with the morning skies—nor would Montaigne
Have noticed them, his mind on other things.
The journey is my heartbeat in this plane.

Yet with more time? Were the excursion longer
To the Cote d'Azur et d'Or, perhaps, La Mer,
The hyacinth fields of Haarlem, Tanganyika,

The river Lethe or the Serpentine,
The Fortunate Isles or Nepal—anywhere,
I might discover what his words still mean:

The journey, in itself, a thing apart.
But no. These words are older than Montaigne's:
The sky is changed. I have not changed my heart.

                                        Helen Bevington

Sympathy

I know what the caged bird feels, alas!
When the sun is bright on the upland slopes;
When the wind stirs soft through the springing grass
And the river flows like a stream of glass;

When the first bird sings and the first bud opes,
And the faint perfume from its chalice steals—
I know what the caged bird feels!

I know why the caged bird beats his wing
Till its blood is red on the cruel bars;
For he must fly back to his perch and cling
When he fain would be on the bough a-swing;
And a pain still throbs in the old, old scars
And they pulse again with a keener sting—
I know why he beats his wing!

I know why the caged bird sings, ah me,
When his wing is bruised and his bosom sore,—
When he beats his bars and would be free;
It is not a carol of joy or glee,
But a prayer that he sends from his deep heart's core,
But a plea, that upward to Heaven he flings—
I know why the caged bird sings!

Paul Laurence Dunbar

To the Man-of-War Bird

Thou who hast slept all night upon the storm,
Waking renew'd on thy prodigious pinions,
(Burst the wild storm? above it thou ascend'st,
And rested on the sky, thy slave that cradled thee,)
Now a blue point, far, far in heaven floating,
As to the light emerging here on deck I watch thee,
(Myself a speck, a point on the world's floating vast.)
Far, far at sea,
After the night's fierce drifts have strewn the shore with wrecks,
With re-appearing day as now so happy and serene,
The rosy and elastic dawn, the flashing sun,
The limpid spread of air cerulean,
Thou also re-appearest.

Thou born to match the gale, (thou art all wings,)
To cope with heaven and earth and sea and hurricane,
Thou ship of air that never furls't thy sails,
Days, even weeks untired and onward, through spaces, realms gyrating
At dusk that look'st on Senegal, at morn America,

That sport'st amid the lightning-flash and thunder-cloud,
In them, in thy experiences, had'st thou my soul,
What joys! What joys were thine!

                                        Walt Whitman

Get Up, Blues

Blues
Never climb a hill
Or sit on a roof
In starlight.

Blues
Just bend low
And moan in the street
And shake a borrowed cup.

Blues
Just sit around
Sipping,
Hatching yesterdays.

Get up, Blues.
Fly.
Learn what it means
To be up high.

                                        James A. Emanuel

HOME, REST AND FINAL VOYAGES

From **Little Gidding**

We shall not cease from exploration
And the end of all our exploring
Will be to arrive where we started
And know the place for the first time.

T. S. Eliot

Into My Heart an Air That Kills

Into my heart an air that kills
     From yon far country blows:
What are those blue remembered hills,
     What spires, what farms are those?

That is the land of lost content,
     I see it shining plain,
The happy highways where I went
     And cannot come again.

A. E. Housman

Love of Country

From "The Lay of the Last Minstrel"

Breathes there the man with soul so dead
Who never to himself hath said:
    "This is my own, my native land"?
Whose heart hath ne'er within him burned
As home his footsteps he hath turned,

47

From wandering on a foreign strand?
If such there breathe, go mark him well;
For him no minstrel raptures swell;
High though his titles, proud his name,
Boundless his wealth as wish can claim;
Despite those titles, power and pelf,
Living, shall forfeit fair renown,
And, doubly dying, shall go down
To the vile dust from whence he sprung,
Unwept, unhonored, and unsung.

Sir Walter Scott

Home-Thoughts, from Abroad

I

Oh, to be in England
Now that April's there,
And whoever wakes in England
Sees, some morning, unaware,
That the lowest boughs and the brushwood sheaf
Round the elm-tree bole are in tiny leaf,
While the chaffinch sings on the orchard bough
In England—now!

II

And after April, when May follows,
And the whitethroat builds, and all the swallows!
Hark, where my blossomed pear-tree in the hedge
Leans to the field and scatters on the clover
Blossoms and dewdrops—at the bent spray's edge—
That's the wise thrush; he sings every song twice over,
Lest you should think he never could recapture
The first fine careless rapture!
And though the fields look rough with hoary dew,
All will be gay when noontide wakes anew
The buttercups, the little children's dower
—Far brighter than this gaudy melon-flower!

Robert Browning

The Tropics in New York

Bananas ripe and green, and ginger root,
   Cocoa in pods and alligator pears,
And tangerines and mangoes and grape fruit,
   Fit for the highest prize at parish fairs.

Set in the window, bringing memories
   Of fruit-trees laden by low-singing rills,
And dewy dawns, and mystical blue skies
   In benediction over nun-like hills.

My eyes grew dim, and I could no more gaze;
   A wave of longing through my body swept,
And, hungry for the old familiar ways,
   I turned aside and bowed my head and wept.

                            Claude McKay

America for Me

'Tis fine to see the Old World, and travel up and down
Among the famous palaces and cities of renown,
To admire the crumbly castles and the statues of the kings,—
But now I think I've had enough of antiquated things.

So it's home again, and home again, America for me!
My heart is turning home again, and there I long to be,
In the land of youth and freedom beyond the ocean bars,
Where the air is full of sunlight and the flag is full of stars.

Oh, London is a man's town, there's power in the air;
And Paris is a woman's town, with flowers in her hair;
And it's sweet to dream in Venice, and it's great to study Rome;
But when it comes to living there is no place like home.

I like the German fir-woods, in green battalions drilled;
I like the gardens of Versailles with flashing fountains filled;
But, oh, to take your hand, my dear, and ramble for a day
In the friendly western woodland where Nature has her way!

I know that Europe's wonderful, yet something seems to lack:
The Past is too much with her, and the people looking back.
But the glory of the Present is to make the Future free,—
We love our land for what she is and what she is to be.

Oh, it's home again, and home again, America for me!
I want a ship that's westward bound to plough the rolling sea,
To the blessed Land of Room Enough beyond the ocean bars,
Where the air is full of sunlight and the flag is full of stars.

Henry Van Dyke

The New Colossus

Not like the brazen giant of Greek fame,
With conquering limbs astride from land to land;
Here at our sea-washed, sunset gates shall stand
A mighty woman with a torch, whose flame
Is the imprisoned lightning, and her name
Mother of Exiles. From her beacon-hand
Glows world-wide welcome; her mild eyes command
The air-bridged harbor that twin cities frame.
"Keep, ancient lands, your storied pomp!" cries she
With silent lips. "Give me your tired, your poor,
Your huddled masses yearning to breathe free,
The wretched refuse of your teeming shore.
Send these, the homeless, tempest-tost to me,
I lift my lamp beside the golden door!"

Emma Lazarus

Home

How brightly glistening in the sun
    The woodland ivy plays!
While yonder beeches from their barks
    Reflect his silver rays.

That sun surveys a lovely scene
    From softly smiling skies;
And wildly through unnumbered trees
    The wind of winter sighs:

Now loud, it thunders o'er my head,
    And now in distance dies.
But give me back my barren hills
    Where colder breezes rise;

Where scarce the scattered, stunted trees
   Can yield an answered swell,
But where a wilderness of heath
   Returns the sound as well.

For yonder garden, fair and wide,
   With groves of evergreen,
Long winding walks, and borders trim,
   And velvet lawns between;

Restore to me that little spot,
   With grey walls compassed round,
Where knotted grass neglected lies,
   And weeds usurp the ground.

Though all around this mansion high
   Invites the foot to roam,
And though its halls are fair within—
   Oh, give me back my HOME!

Anne Brontë

The Long Voyage

Not that the pines are darker there,
nor mid-May dogwood brighter there,
nor swifts more swift in summer air;
   it was my own country,

having its thunderclap of spring,
its long midsummer ripening,
its corn hoar-stiff at harvesting,
   almost like any country,

yet being mine; its face, its speech,
its hills bent low within my reach,
its river birch and upland beech
   were mine, of my own country.

Now the dark waters at the bow
fold back, like earth against the plow;
foam brightens like the dogwood now
   at home, in my own country.

Malcolm Cowley

Home, Sweet Home!

'Mid pleasures and palaces though we may roam,
Be it ever so humble, there's no place like home.
A charm from the sky seems to hallow us there,
Which, seek through the world, is ne'er met with elsewhere.
  Home! sweet home!
  There's no place like home!

An exile from home, splendour dazzles in vain!
Oh! give me my lowly thatch'd cottage again!
The birds singing gaily that came at my call,
Give me them, with the peace of mind DEARER than all!
  Home! sweet home!
  There's no place like home!

John Howard Payne

Anchored

If thro' the sea of night which
  here surrounds me,
 I could swim out beyond the
  farthest star,
Break every barrier of circumstance
  that bounds me,
 And greet the Sun of sweeter
  life afar,

Tho' near you there is passion,
  grief, and sorrow,
 And out there rest and joy and
  peace and all,
I should renounce that beckoning
  for to-morrow,
 I could not choose to go beyond
  your call.

Paul Laurence Dunbar

Terminus

It is time to be old,
To take in sail
The god of bounds,
Who sets to seas a shore,
Came to me in his fatal rounds,
And said: "No more!
No farther shoot
Thy broad ambitious branches, and thy root.
Fancy departs: no more invent,
Contract thy firmament
To compass of a tent.
There's not enough of this and that,
Make thy option which of two;
Economize the failing river,
Not the less revere the Giver,
Leave the many and hold the few.
Timely wise accept the terms,
Soften the fall with wary foot;
A little while
Still plan and smile,
And fault of novel germs
Mature the unfallen fruit.
Curse, if thou wilt, thy sires,
Bad husbands of their fires,
Who, when they gave thee breath,
Failed to bequeath
The needful sinew stark as once,
The Baresark marrow to thy bones,
But left a legacy of ebbing veins,
Inconstant heat and nerveless reins,
Amid the Muses, left thee deaf and dumb,
Amid the gladiators, halt and numb."

As the bird trims her to the gale,
I trim myself to the storm of time,
I man the rudder, reef the sail,
Obey the voice at eve obeyed at prime:
"Lowly faithful, banish fear,
Right onward drive unharmed;
The port, well worth the cruise, is near,
And every wave is charmed."

                                        Ralph Waldo Emerson

The Tramps

Can you recall, dear comrade, when we tramped God's land together,
And we sang the old, old Earth-song, for our youth was very sweet;
When we drank and fought and lusted, as we mocked at tie and
    tether,
Along the road to Anywhere, the wide world at our feet—

Along the road to Anywhere, when each day had its story;
   When time was yet our vassal, and life's jest was still unstale;
When peace unfathomed filled our hearts as, bathed in amber glory,
   Along the road to Anywhere we watched the sunsets pale?

Alas! the road to Anywhere is pitfalled with disaster;
   There's hunger, want, and weariness, yet O we loved it so!
As on we tramped exultantly, and no man was our master,
   And no man guessed what dreams were ours, as, swinging heel and
     toe,
We tramped the road to Anywhere, the magic road to Anywhere,
The tragic road to Anywhere, such dear, dim years ago.

Robert Service

Heart o' the North

And when I come to the dim trail-end,
   I who have been Life's rover,
This is all I would ask, my friend,
   Over and over and over:

A little space on a stony hill
   With never another near me,
Sky o' the North that's vast and still,
   With a single star to cheer me;

Star that gleams on a moss-grey stone
   Graven by those who love me—
There would I lie alone, alone,
   With a single pine above me;

Pine that the north wind whinnies through—
   Oh, I have been Life's lover!
But there I'd lie and listen to
   Eternity passing over.

Robert Service

Requiem

Under the wide and starry sky
   Dig the grave and let me lie:
Glad did I live and gladly die,
   And I laid me down with a will.

This be the verse you grave for me:
Here he lies where he long'd to be;
Home is the sailor, home from the sea,
And the hunter home from the hill.

Robert Louis Stevenson

Tavern

I'll keep a little tavern
   Below the high hill's crest,
Wherein all grey-eyed people
   May set them down and rest.

There shall be plates a-plenty,
   And mugs to melt the chill
Of all the grey-eyed people
   Who happen up the hill.

There sound will sleep the traveller,
   And dream his journey's end,
But I will rouse at midnight
   The falling fire to tend.

Aye, 'tis a curious fancy—
   But all the good I know
Was taught me out of two grey eyes
   A long time ago.

Edna St. Vincent Millay

Up-Hill

Does the road wind uphill all the way?
   Yes, to the very end.
Will the day's journey take the whole long day?
   From morn to night, my friend.

But is there for the night a resting-place?
　　A roof for when the slow, dark hours begin,
May not the darkness hide it from my face?
　　You cannot miss that inn.

Shall I meet other wayfarers at night?
　　Those who have gone before.
Then must I knock, or call when just in sight?
　　They will not keep you waiting at that door.

Shall I find comfort, travel-sore and weak?
　　Of labour you shall find the sum.
Will there be beds for me and all who seek?
　　Yea, beds for all who come.

Christina Rossetti

The Listeners

"Is there anybody there?" said the Traveler,
　　Knocking on the moonlit door;
And his horse in the silence champed the grasses
　　Of the forest's ferny floor:
And a bird flew up out of the turret,
　　Above the Traveler's head:
And he smote upon the door again a second time;
　　"Is there anybody there?" he said.
But no one descended to the Traveler;
　　No head from the leaf-fringed sill
Leaned over and looked into his gray eyes,
　　Where he stood perplexed and still.
But only a host of phantom listeners
　　That dwelt in the lone house then
Stood listening in the quiet of the moonlight
　　To that voice from the world of men:
Stood thronging the faint moonbeams on the dark stair,
　　That goes down to the empty hall,
Hearkening in an air stirred and shaken
　　By the lonely Traveler's call.
And he felt in his heart their strangeness,
　　Their stillness answering his cry,
While his horse moved, cropping the dark turf,
　　'Neath the starred and leafy sky;
For he suddenly smote on the door, even

Louder, and lifted his head: —
"Tell them I came, and no one answered,
    That I kept my word," he said.
Never the least stir made the listeners,
    Though every word he spake
Fell echoing through the shadowiness of the still house
    From the one man left awake:
Ay, they heard his foot upon the stirrup,
    And the sound of iron on stone,
And how the silence surged softly backward,
    When the plunging hoofs were gone.

Walter de la Mare

Dream-Land

By a route obscure and lonely,
Haunted by ill angels only,
Where an Eidolon, named NIGHT,
On a black throne reigns upright,
    I have reached these lands but newly
        From an ultimate dim Thule —
From a wild weird clime that lieth, sublime,
        Out of SPACE — out of TIME.

Bottomless vales and boundless floods,
And chasms, and caves and Titan woods,
With forms that no man can discover
For the tears that drip all over;
Mountains toppling evermore
Into seas without a shore;
Seas that restlessly aspire,
Surging, unto skies of fire;
Lakes that endlessly outspread
Their lone waters — lone and dead, —
Their still waters — still and chilly
With the snows of the lolling lily.

By the lakes that thus outspread
Their lone waters, lone and dead, —
Their sad waters, sad and chilly
With the snows of the lolling lily, —
By the mountains — near the river
Murmuring lowly, murmuring ever, —

By the grey woods,—by the swamp
Where the toad and the newt encamp,—
By the dismal tarns and pools
   Where dwell the Ghouls,—
By each spot the most unholy—
In each nook most melancholy,—
There the traveller meets, aghast,
Sheeted Memories of the Past—
Shrouded forms that start and sigh
As they pass the wanderer by—
White-robed forms of friends long given,
In agony, to the Earth—and Heaven.

For the heart whose woes are legion
'T is a peaceful, soothing region—
For the spirit that walks in shadow
'T is—oh 't is an Eldorado!
But the traveller, travelling through it,
May not—dare not openly view it;
Never its mysteries are exposed
To the weak human eye unclosed;
So wills its King, who hath forbid
The uplifting of the fringéd lid;
And thus the sad Soul that here passes
Beholds it but through darkened glasses.

By a route obscure and lonely,
Haunted by ill angels only,
Where an Eidolon, named NIGHT,
On a black throne reigns upright,
I have wandered home but newly
From this ultimate dim Thule.

                                    Edgar Allan Poe

The Chariot

Because I could not stop for Death,
He kindly stopped for me;
The carriage held but just ourselves
And Immortality.

We slowly drove, he knew no haste,
And I had put away

My labor, and my leisure too,
For his civility.

We passed the school where children played,
Their lessons scarcely done;
We passed the fields of gazing grain,
We passed the setting sun.

We paused before a house that seemed
A swelling of the ground;
The roof was scarcely visible,
The cornice but a mound.

Since then 'tis centuries; but each
Feels shorter than the day
I first surmised the horses' heads
Were toward eternity.

                                        Emily Dickinson

Heaven-Haven

I have desired to go
        Where springs not fail,
To fields where flies no sharp and sided hail
And a few lilies blow.

And I have asked to be
        Where no storms come,
Where the green swell is in the havens dumb,
And out of the swing of the sea.

                                Gerard Manley Hopkins

Dream Land

Where sunless rivers weep
Their waves into the deep,
She sleeps a charmed sleep:
        Awake her not.
Led by a single star,
She came from very far
To seek where shadows are
        Her pleasant lot.

She left the rosy morn,
She left the fields of corn,
For twilight cold and lorn
   And water springs.
Through sleep, as through a veil,
She sees the sky look pale,
And hears the nightingale
   That sadly sings.

Rest, rest, a perfect rest
Shed over brow and breast;
Her face is toward the west,
   The purple land.
She cannot see the grain
Ripening on hill and plain;
She cannot feel the rain
   Upon her hand.

Rest, rest, for evermore
Upon a mossy shore;
Rest, rest at the heart's core
   Till time shall cease:
Sleep that no pain shall wake,
Night that no morn shall break
Till joy shall overtake
   Her perfect peace.

Christina Rossetti

Ozymandias

I met a traveler from an antique land
Who said: Two vast and trunkless legs of stone
Stand in the desert. Near them, on the sand,
Half sunk, a shattered visage lies, whose frown,
And wrinkled lip, and sneer of cold command,
Tell that its sculptor well those passions read
Which yet survive, stamped on these lifeless things,
The hand that mocked them and the heart that fed;
And on the pedestal these words appear:
"My name is Ozymandias, king of kings:
Look on my works, ye Mighty, and despair!"
Nothing beside remains. Round the decay

Of that colossal wreck, boundless and bare
The lone and level sands stretch far away.

Percy Bysshe Shelley

Crossing the Bar

Sunset and evening star,
    And one clear call for me!
And may there be no moaning of the bar,
    When I put out to sea,

But such a tide as moving seems asleep,
    Too full for sound and foam,
When that which drew from out the boundless deep
    Turns again home.

Twilight and evening bell,
    And after that the dark!
And may there be no sadness of farewell,
    When I embark;

For though from out our bourne of Time and Place
    The flood may bear me far,
I hope to see my Pilot face to face
    When I have crossed the bar.

Alfred, Lord Tennyson

Index of Authors, Titles and First Lines
Titles, in italics, are given only when distinct from first lines.